LET'S FIX LUNCH!

stasher

Let's Fix Lunch!

Enjoy Delicious, Planet-Friendly
Meals at Work, School,
or On the Go

KAT NOURI, Founder of Stasher Bags

Recipe contributions from **SANDRA WU**
Photography by **ERIN SCOTT**

CHRONICLE BOOKS
SAN FRANCISCO

Library of Congress Cataloging-in-Publication
Data available.

ISBN: 978-1-7972-0573-1

Manufactured in China.

Recipe contributions from Sandra Wu.
Photo direction by Stacie Navarro.
Food styling by Lillian Kang.
Prop styling by Claire Mack.
Design by Lizzie Vaughan.
Typesetting by Taylor Roy.
Typeset in Avenir and Alda.

10 9 8 7 6 5 4 3 2 1

Chronicle books and gifts are available at special
quantity discounts to corporations, professional
associations, literacy programs, and other
organizations. For details and discount information,
please contact our premiums department at
corporatesales@chroniclebooks.com or at
1-800-759-0190.

Chronicle Books LLC
680 Second Street
San Francisco, California 94107
www.chroniclebooks.com

This book is dedicated to the Stasher Squad—
everyone, everywhere who chooses to rethink
single-use plastic and leave our planet a better place.

ALL IT TAKES IS ONE.

One good call, one day at a time.

Then another one. And another one.

This is how we make real change.

Because we only have one planet.

And it's up to all of us to save it.

And when we all work together,

amazing things happen.

We all have something to give.

To save. To protect.

We all have our reasons.

And they all count. We can all

SAVE WHAT MATTERS.

CONTENTS

THE GOOD NEWS

A NOTE FROM STASHER'S FOUNDER, KAT NOURI

Dear you,

Here's the good news: Even though it feels as if everywhere we turn there's not-so-great news about the environment, climate change, and the plight of the planet, there's actually lots of good news! Some days we have to look a little harder for it, but trust me, it's everywhere. For starters, you're reading this—a note written to you—which means you've already done a good deed by purchasing this book. Because for every copy sold of *Let's Fix Lunch*, Stasher will donate to No Kid Hungry, an organization that provides meals to kids and helps them get the healthy food they need. The many small choices we each make can add up to a big impact for people and for Planet Earth. By using any of the tips and recipes in the following pages, you'll be making smart choices for yourself, your family, and the planet. Go, you!

As for me, I grew up with a nutritionist for a mom and a world-class athlete for a dad, so my childhood kitchen in Iran was full of fresh ingredients and healthy family recipes (check out the Kuku Sabzi (Persian Herb Frittata) on page 43 for a family favorite!). Fast-forward to today, and food is still more than just a meal—it's a way to nurture family and friends.

When I started Stasher, I was tired of the plastic waste chok-ing the planet and frankly pretty tired of packing my kids' healthy lunches in stuff that turned into trash just a few hours later. As a curious entrepreneur, my gears are always turning. And I decided there had to be a business that could nurture the planet too.

Along the way, I had to break a whole lot of rules and do things I was told were "impossible" (a word that should always be put in air quotes, if you ask me), but the result is Stasher—the first endlessly reusable bag, which has already prevented nearly 1 billion single-use plastics from piling up in landfills and polluting our oceans. And, for every Stasher purchased, we donate to nonprofit organizations that help make the planet better than we found it.

We created this cookbook to show how delicious and easy it is to make a big difference, starting with small choices in the kitchen. Whether you want to prep healthy meals to save time and money, or use fewer disposables when you cook, you don't have to overhaul your entire existence to make positive change.

Why lunch? Simple!

Not many of us eat lunch at home, which means we're pack-ing meals, eating out, or ordering takeout. Recent research shows that plastic food containers of all types are one of the biggest contributors to our growing global waste problem. A UK study identified the "lunch on the go" habit as the source of nearly 11 billion packaging waste items per year—and it's on the rise, with 65 percent more of us getting takeout and delivery compared to 5 years ago.

School lunches are another big contributor to the global waste problem, thanks to plastic bags and other wraps that are used and discarded in the same day. Prepackaged items, like granola bars, chips, and yogurt in plastic tubes, are high in convenience but even higher in plastic waste. In fact, the Environmental Protection Agency (EPA) recently identified that plastic food packaging makes up about 45 percent of landfill waste in the United States. Forty. Five. Percent.

Back to the good news! In this book, you'll find tips on how to avoid single-use plastic as well as reduce food waste. Bonus? You'll save money! We've also included ways to shop smarter, prep faster, and waste less of everything. By the time you've lunched your way through these recipes, you'll have added over 30 ideas to your eco-friendly arsenal.

It's that easy—and that important.

Habits aren't created overnight. Good or bad, we have to do things repeatedly for them to stick. So pat yourself on the back every time you use a reusable nonplastic container instead of a single-use baggie, a metal straw instead of a plastic one, or a thermos instead of a to-go coffee cup. And when you forget, give yourself a break and get back on the horse. We're playing the long game here, and it's not about being perfect (spoiler alert: nobody is).

The plastic-free movement is about sharing our ideas, encouraging one another, and getting creative—and it succeeds when we stay inspired. Across the Stasher offices, we're always gushing over users' ingenious, crafty, clever uses for Stasher bags and are constantly on the lookout for tips and tricks to reduce our own waste. So let's stay connected and keep chatting!

Please consider this cookbook a huge thanks for every good choice you've made for our planet. Change won't take just a village—it'll take all our villages. But together, we can do anything. And that's great news.

Happy cooking!

—*Kat*

LITTLE CHOICES, BIG CHANGE:

FOUNDATIONAL TIPS FOR WASTE-FREE MEALS

We've all experienced the power of small things—like how a kind word from a friend can make your whole day, or how the tiny pebble in your shoe can give you a mean blister. Turns out, this is also true on a global scale.

Small in size but many in number, single-use plastics have created a big, planet-size problem. It's everywhere—from the plastic wrap on produce, to plastic takeout containers, to the granola bar wrappers and chip bags stuffed in lunch boxes every day.

We know we have to do something, but the idea that we have to change everything, right now, in order to save our oceans and our lands can be downright overwhelming.

Thankfully, we have the brilliance of *one*. The plastic-free movement is fueled by one choice, one day at a time, one person at a time to save the one planet we've got. And here at Stasher, of all the steps we can take, our favorite one is what we like to call "Litter-Free Lunch."

A litter-free lunch doesn't require you to drop a huge wad of cash replacing the entire contents of your pantry. And it certainly doesn't mean losing precious sleep in the morning to prep a gourmet meal. In fact, you probably have most of what you need to make this habit a reality.

Aren't you getting hungry just thinking about it?

THE LUNCH FACTOR

You may be wondering why this book focuses on lunch and not a bigger meal, like dinner. Well, check out these trashy stats: Recent research shows that plastic containers used to hold food—from to-go containers to plastic baggies—are one of the biggest contributors to plastic waste. Even if you're tossing your to-go container in the recycling bin, it's not guaranteed to actually be recycled.

Hard-to-recycle items, like black plastic takeout containers, can throw off optical sorters that separate materials for recycling plants. Containers soiled by food are eliminated from the recycling process altogether and sent to the landfill. And those baggies? The average consumer uses between 200 and 1,000 of them per year, most of which end up in the ocean or a landfill.

And that's just takeout. According to Oklahoma State University, elementary school lunches are estimated to generate about 67 pounds [30 kg] of waste per student per year, which includes food and plastic waste coming from packaging and single-use baggies.

Schools are taking notice of the waste and the high costs to manage it. Some have chosen to ban single-use plastics, while others simply send the waste back home. If you've ever opened your kids' lunch box and wondered why your child never seems to throw away the used wrappers, peels, and juice box containers, it's probably because your school is reducing the amount of waste they produce to keep costs down.

For a meal that's dealt such a blow to the planet, lunch tends to be something we phone in. But you can change that.

GETTING STARTED

Before you dive into the recipes, here is a list of items that will help you reduce waste in your kitchen so that you can make litter-free lunches every day of the week. If you have good secondhand stores in your area, check out what's available there. Reducing waste shouldn't break the bank. And by choosing perfectly good used products, you're reusing something that's already in the world!

REUSABLE UTENSILS
Wash and reuse the ones you already have at home instead of buying new.

STRAWS
Choose compostable straws (they come in larger packs these days, and are perfect for kiddos).

REUSABLE NAPKINS
Hand towels will also do the trick and can be used multiple times before needing to go in the wash.

REUSABLE WATER BOTTLES
If you don't already have a reusable water bottle, reach for a mason jar—they're easy to find used.

A LUNCH BAG
If you've got a refrigerator available at work, you don't really need an insulated lunch bag—just toss your food items in any reusable bag you have on hand. Or check out your local thrift store (bonus points for vintage vibes).

A THERMOS
An insulated, vacuum-sealed container allows you to pack and enjoy hot foods and soups.

A HARD-SIDED CONTAINER
Choose glass containers instead of plastic if you're planning to reheat food (as plastic can release chemicals into food when heated), or use a ceramic plate in the microwave.

FOOD STORAGE BAGS

Food-grade silicone Stasher bags are the perfect replacement for single-use plastic. One Stasher bag is endlessly reusable and can replace hundreds, even thousands of plastic waste items per year depending on how often you're using it. Store sandwiches, fruits, veggies, and other lunch items without creating more trash.

FOOD WRAPS

Beeswax wraps are a great natural replacement for anything you'd otherwise wrap in plastic, such as sandwiches, bread, or cheese.

GO NAKED

Ask yourself if your lunch really needs to be wrapped. Lunch boxes are designed for easy cleaning, so consider whether a rice cake or crackers really need an extra wrap, or whether they'll be fine loose for an hour or two before you enjoy them.

AT-A-GLANCE ICONS

As you make your way through the snacks and dishes in this book, you'll see icons at the top of each recipe page. These icons are designed to make it easy to choose what recipe works best for you. You'll see icons for:

VEGETARIAN

These recipes use only vegetarian ingredients, or include a vegetarian variation.

FREEZABLE

These dishes can be prepped ahead of time and stored in the freezer.

SCHOOL-LUNCH FRIENDLY

These recipes are designed to be kid friendly, or include a kid-friendly variation.

MAKE AHEAD

These dishes can be prepped ahead of time and packed in Stasher bags or other reusable containers.

BUILDING BLOCKS

These recipes utilize building block ingredients outlined in A Guide to Make-Ahead Ingredients (pages 23–35).

With the tools, tips, and tricks outlined in these pages, you'll have everything you need to start making litter-free lunches!

A GUIDE TO MAKE-AHEAD INGREDIENTS:

BUILDING BLOCKS FOR EASY MEAL PREP THROUGHOUT THE WEEK

The easier it is to make a litter-free lunch, the more likely it is to become a habit. That's why we've designed this book to be as user friendly and simple to use as possible. This section includes simple ideas on how to shop smarter, prep faster, and waste less of everything, with building blocks that form the foundation of many of the recipes in the pages ahead.

Lettuces

Wash and spin-dry a day or two in advance and store in a Stasher bag or container lined with paper towels.

Hearty Greens

Kale, chard, collard greens, mustard greens, and other hearty greens can be washed and prepped a few days in advance. Wash the greens in several changes of water, then remove the stems and cut the leaves into strips (thicker ones for cooking, thinner ones for raw use in salads). Spin-dry and store in a Stasher bag or container lined with paper towels.

They can be cooked a day or two in advance too: sautéed in a bit of olive oil, or blanched and squeezed dry for use in recipes.

Grains

The following easy-to-find grains form the foundation of the bowl recipes in this book, but this list is only a small example of what you can use in your lunch-making endeavors.

MEDIUM- OR SHORT-GRAIN WHITE RICE
Rinse 1 cup [200 g] of rice in a sieve under cold running water. In a medium saucepan, combine the rice, 1¼ cups [300 ml] of water, and ½ tsp of kosher salt (optional). Let stand for 30 minutes. Bring to a boil over medium-high heat, stir, and distribute the grains in an even layer. Turn the heat down to low and cook, covered, until the rice is tender and has absorbed the water, about 13 minutes. Remove the pan from the heat and let stand for 15 minutes. Stir the rice with a wooden spoon, scraping along the sides and bottom of the pot. Makes about 3 cups [440 g].

LONG-GRAIN WHITE RICE

Rinse 1 cup [200 g] of rice in a sieve under cold running water. In a medium saucepan, combine the rice, 1½ cups [360 ml] of water, and ½ tsp of kosher salt (optional). Bring to a boil over medium-high heat, stirring once or twice. Turn down the heat to low, and cook, covered, until the rice is tender and has absorbed the water, about 15 minutes. Remove the pan from the heat and let stand for 10 minutes, then fluff the grains with a fork. Makes about 3½ cups [470 g].

BROWN RICE (LONG- OR SHORT-GRAIN)

Bring 10 cups [2.3 L] of water to a boil in a large saucepan. Rinse 1 cup [200 g] of brown rice in a sieve under cold running water. Add the rice and ½ tsp of kosher salt (optional) and boil, uncovered, until tender, about 30 minutes. Drain well in a colander. Makes 2½ cups [410 g].

QUINOA

Rinse 1 cup [180 g] of quinoa in a fine-mesh sieve under cold running water. In a medium saucepan, combine the quinoa, 1½ cups [360 ml] of water, and ½ tsp of kosher salt, and bring to a boil over medium-high heat. Turn down the heat to low and simmer, covered, until the quinoa is tender and has absorbed the water, about 20 minutes. Remove from heat and let stand for 5 minutes. Fluff with a fork. Makes about 3½ cups [420 g].

TIP *To quickly cool cooked grains, greens, pasta, lentils (anything, really!) before packing them up, spread them out on a baking sheet in a thin layer.*

Pasta

Cook to al dente according to package instructions, drain in a colander, rinse with cold water, shake dry, and drizzle with olive oil to prevent sticking. Store in a Stasher bag or container and refrigerate for 3 to 5 days.

Hard-Boiled Eggs

Stasher's office manager (a.k.a. Chief Sustenance Officer), Allison, is the queen of perfect hard-boiled eggs. Here, she shares the secret to her delicious results: Fill a saucepan with enough water to ensure the eggs will be covered with at least 1 in [2.5 cm] of water. Bring to a boil over high heat. Using a slotted spoon or wire skimmer, gently add only as many eggs as will fit in a single layer. Lower the heat and maintain a gentle rolling boil for 11 minutes. Remove the eggs from the water and gently submerge them in a bowl of ice water to cool. Unpeeled, the eggs will keep in the refrigerator for up to 1 week.

Lentils

Red lentils break down easily and are best saved for soups and curries. For lentils that keep their shape and perform well in salads and grain bowls, use the green or brown varieties.

Sort through 1 cup [200 g] of green or brown lentils and remove any debris. Rinse in a sieve under cold running water, then place in a medium saucepan with 3 cups [720 ml] of water. Bring to a boil, then turn the heat down to medium-low and simmer, partially covered, until tender, 25 to 30 minutes. Drain in a colander, drizzle with olive oil, and season with salt. Makes about 2½ cups [435 g].

Roasted Vegetables

A wide variety of vegetables benefit from roasting in the oven. Because this technique is largely hands-off and two to three trays can be going at once, it's a great method to employ when prepping ingredients on a Sunday for the week ahead.

Preheat the oven to 425°F [220°C]. For easy cleanup, line a rimmed baking sheet with parchment paper or a silicone baking mat. Cut the vegetables into strips or bite-size pieces, toss with olive oil, salt, and pepper, and arrange in a single layer on the prepared baking sheet. Be sure to leave some room between the vegetable pieces so they don't end up steaming instead of roasting.

If you're roasting more than one type of vegetable per sheet, divide the sheet into sections so the vegetables can be easily removed as they are done cooking. Roast to desired doneness, which will range from 10 to 30 minutes depending on the size and type of vegetable. These simply prepared vegetables will keep in the refrigerator for 3 to 5 days, ready to be flavored in a multitude of ways.

Blanched Vegetables

For vegetables that don't need extra browning and caramel-ization (greens, peas, corn, and green beans, for example), try blanching (cooking in a large amount of salted water until just tender) instead. Cook one type of vegetable at a time, slipping them into an ice bath to cool quickly as they finish cooking. Drain the vegetables on a dish towel–lined rimmed baking sheet before packing them up in a damp paper towel–lined Stasher bag or container.

Beans & Chickpeas

Canned beans and chickpeas are easy pantry staples to keep around for last-minute protein add-ins: Simply rinse and drain well in a colander before using them in your favorite recipes. Transfer any leftovers to a Stasher bag or sealed container; they will keep, refrigerated, for up to 5 days.

To skip the can, use dried beans and cook according to package directions, which often include an overnight soak. Cooked beans and cooked chickpeas will keep in the refrigerator for 3 to 4 days.

Nuts & Seeds

Both raw and toasted nuts and seeds are great to have on hand to add extra protein, fat, and crunch to salads, sandwiches, grain bowls, and snacks. Raw nuts and seeds provide the most flexibility, while pre-roasted versions are great for convenience.

Small amounts of chopped nuts or seeds can be toasted over medium heat on the stove top, but for more even browning and less hands-on work, toast them on a baking sheet in a 350°F [180°C] oven. Toast, stirring once or twice, for 6 to 10 minutes, until evenly browned and with a rich, nutty aroma. No matter the method used, transfer the toasted nuts or seeds to a large plate or cool baking sheet to stop them from continuing to cook. Transfer any leftovers to a Stasher bag or sealed container; they will keep, at room temperature, for up to 1 week.

Baked Tofu

These chewy, savory nuggets are an excellent make-ahead protein option for meatless lunches.

Preheat the oven to 400°F [200°C]. Line a baking sheet with parchment paper.

Cut one 14 to 16 oz [400 to 455 g] block of extra-firm tofu into 1 in [2.5 cm] slabs. Place a double layer of paper towels onto a baking sheet and arrange the tofu slabs in a single layer on top. Cover with a double layer of paper towels and set another baking sheet on top. Place a heavy cast-iron skillet or several large cans onto the baking sheet to weigh it down for 20 minutes.

Meanwhile, in a large bowl, whisk together 3 Tbsp of soy sauce, 1 Tbsp of sesame oil, and 1 Tbsp of maple syrup. Cut the pressed tofu into 1 in [2.5 cm] cubes, gently toss in the marinade, and let sit for several minutes.

Arrange the tofu in a single layer onto the prepared baking sheet and bake until lightly browned, about 30 minutes, turning the pieces over halfway through baking. Makes about 2 cups [320 g].

Roast Chicken

For the best price per pound and less waste (plus an entire carcass and bones to use for homemade chicken stock), buy whole chickens rather than individual pieces. Cut a 4 to 4½ lb [1.8 to 2 kg] chicken into the following pieces: wings, thighs, drumsticks, breasts, and backbone. Pat dry, drizzle lightly with olive oil, then salt generously. Roast in a 400°F [200°C] oven on a baking sheet until the thickest part of the breast registers 160°F [75°C] on an instant-read thermometer and the thighs and drumsticks register 175°F [80°C], 30 to 40 minutes. The wings and backbone will be done when they are golden brown and crisp, about 25 minutes (save these for use in stock). Adjust the baking time for smaller or larger chickens.

Chicken Stock

By making stock at home from reserved vegetable scraps, you'll reduce both your food waste and disposable packaging. In a large pot or Dutch oven over high heat, combine about 1¼ lb [570 g] of reserved carcass pieces from a roast chicken, 2 cups [280 g] of roughly chopped vegetable scraps, 2 garlic cloves, 1 small handful of parsley stems, 1 bay leaf, 1 sprig of thyme, and 5 black peppercorns. Cover with 8 cups [2 L] of water.

Bring to a boil, skimming occasionally, then lower the heat to medium. Cook, partially covered, for 1 hour, adjusting the heat as needed to maintain a lively simmer.

Strain through a fine-mesh sieve into a large heatproof bowl or another pot. Discard the solids. You should have 4 to 5 cups [960 ml to 1.2 L] of stock. Place the pot of strained stock into a sink filled with ice water until cool, stirring occasionally. Transfer to a sealed container or Stasher bag and refrigerate for up to 5 days, or freeze for up to 3 months.

Vinaigrettes

Use the following basic formula to work from when coming up with your own homemade vinaigrettes: ¼ cup [60 ml] acid (citrus juice, vinegar, verjus, or a combination) + ½ cup [120 ml] oil + 1 tsp kosher salt + 2 tsp sweetener (optional).

Add-ins, such as minced aromatics (shallot, garlic, ginger), spices, fresh chopped herbs, mustard, and grated citrus zest, are a great way to further customize flavor.

SAMPLE MENUS USING BUILDING BLOCKS

SUNDAY PREP	MONDAY	TUESDAY
Roast chicken	Chicken Caesar Salad with Parmesan Croutons (page 77)	Chicken Noodle Soup (page 81)
Roast vegetables	Hummus & Roasted Veggie Wraps (page 99)	Frittata: Fold roasted veggies into a frittata or quiche (use a store-bought piecrust to keep it super easy!)
Chickpeas	Hummus & Roasted Veggie Wraps (page 99)	Chickpea Waldorf Salad on Lavash (page 94)
Cooked lentils	Kale Salad with Apples, Lentils, Feta & Seeds (page 85)	Lentil Soup: Sauté chopped yellow onion in olive oil until softened. Add chopped kale, crushed tomatoes, cooked lentils, water (as needed), salt, pepper, and a pinch each of basil and oregano. Bring to a boil, then simmer for 10 minutes.
Cooked rice or quinoa	Vegetarian Quinoa Bibimbap Bowl (page 122)	Sauté a mix of veggies until bright and fragrant; add chicken stock and rice/quinoa for an easy veggie soup.
Hard-boiled eggs	Cobb Salad with Chicken & Avocado Dressing (page 82)	Chop them up and mix with plain yogurt or mayonnaise, minced shallot, lemon, salt, and dill. Add a dollop onto toast for an open-faced egg salad sandwich.
Baked tofu	Baked Tofu Salad with Miso-Sesame Vinaigrette (page 75)	Vegetarian Quinoa Bibimbap Bowl (page 122)
Romaine and kale, washed and chopped	Kale Salad with Apples, Lentils, Feta & Seeds (page 85)	Brown Rice, Lentils & Greens Bowl with Glazed Cashews (page 119)
Cooked pasta	Chicken Noodle Soup (page 81)	Tuna Pesto Pasta Salad with Tomatoes & Beans (page 112)

WEDNESDAY

Cobb Salad with Chicken & Avocado Dressing (page 82)

Salad: Place roasted veggies over a mix of greens, like romaine, kale, and arugula. Add feta or goat cheese, sliced almonds, and toss with Avocado Dressing (page 82).

Use chickpeas in place of lentils in the Brown Rice, Lentils & Greens Bowl with Glazed Cashews (page 119).

Brown Rice, Lentils & Greens Bowl with Glazed Cashews (page 119)

Act 2 Fried Rice (page 111)

Layer slices of hard-boiled egg with avocado, tomato, bacon, and cheese on brioche, for a take on a breakfast sandwich.

Tofu-Veggie Wrap: Spread a tortilla with simple peanut sauce (combining creamy peanut butter with a small amount of hoisin sauce and sriracha). Add sliced carrots, cucumber, red pepper, and tofu.

Chicken Fajita Bowl (page 116)

Sauté crumbled pork sausage and diced onion in olive oil. Add strips of kale or Swiss chard and sauté until tender. Stir in pasta to reheat. Top with Parmesan before serving.

THURSDAY

Pesto Chicken Sandwich (page 93)

Chicken Fajita Bowl (page 116)

Use chickpeas instead of chicken in the Chicken Caesar Salad (page 77).

Toss lentils with a vinaigrette dressing (page 33) and make into a meatless Nicoise salad with salad greens, cherry tomatoes, roasted potatoes, and blanched green beans.

Brown Rice, Lentils & Greens Bowl with Glazed Cashews (page 119)

Eat as is, as a snack, with salt to taste. Perhaps alongside a bright, fresh salad, like the Chicken Caesar Salad with Parmesan Croutons (page 77).

Tofu Noodle Bowl: Top cooked and cooled rice or soba noodles with tofu, shredded cabbage, cooked shelled edamame, and cucumber slices. Serve with Miso-Sesame Vinaigrette (page 75) drizzled on top.

Cobb Salad with Chicken & Avocado Dressing (page 82)

Orzo with Ham & Buttered Peas (page 115). Orzo can be replaced with another type of pasta.

FRIDAY

Chicken Fajita Bowl (page 116)

Hash: Roast chopped potatoes, add additional warmed, roasted veggies, and top with a fried egg.

Spread leftover hummus on thick cut toast and top with slices of avocado, hard-boiled egg, and paprika.

Mix lentils with a store-bought curry sauce. Add baby spinach and cook until just wilted. Serve over rice (see instructions on page 27 for long-grain rice).

Use whatever's leftover in tacos, quinoa fritters, or rice pudding.

Make deviled eggs with any leftovers as a weekend treat!

Act 2 Fried Rice (page 111)

Breakfast Smoothie: Use the extra greens in a breakfast smoothie with banana, frozen pineapple, plain yogurt, and coconut water.

Kid-friendly variation of Italian Tomato-Bread Soup (page 88)

Litter-Free Lunches

Easy, Delicious Recipes That Are
Good to Eat & Good for the Planet

ON-THE-GO SNACKS

Healthy, Packable Bites for Midday Munchies

MAKES 8 CUPS [750 G]

Sesame-Coconut Granola

 Vegetarian   Make Ahead   Building Blocks   School-Lunch Friendly

½ cup [120 ml] maple syrup

¼ cup [55 g] tahini

2 Tbsp extra-virgin olive oil

1 tsp ground cinnamon

1 tsp kosher salt

3 cups [300 g] old-fashioned rolled oats

1 cup [95 g] unsweetened shredded coconut

1 cup [140 g] raw pepitas

¼ cup [40 g] flaxseed

¼ cup [35 g] sesame seeds

Preheat the oven to 325°F [165°C]. Grease the bottom and sides of a 9 by 13 in [23 by 33 cm] baking dish and line with parchment paper.

In a large bowl, whisk together the maple syrup, tahini, olive oil, cinnamon, and salt until smooth.

Add the oats, coconut, pepitas, flaxseed, and sesame seeds and stir until evenly coated. Spread the mixture into the prepared pan. Use a spatula to press down firmly to form an even and compact layer.

Bake until the granola is golden brown and fragrant, about 40 minutes, rotating the pan halfway through baking. Let cool completely in the pan, then invert the granola onto a baking sheet. Peel off the parchment paper and break the granola into clusters. Store the granola in an airtight container for up to 2 weeks.

ECO TIP Fresh, seasonal herbs can be processed in a food processor and then frozen into ice cubes. Store the cubes in a Stasher or freezer bag so you can add flavorful herbs to your dishes all year long.

MAKES 16 SQUARES

Kuku Sabzi (Persian Herb Frittata)

 Vegetarian   Make Ahead   School-Lunch Friendly

4 Tbsp [60 ml] extra-virgin olive oil

5 oz [140 g] chopped baby spinach (about 4 cups)

3 cups [145 g] thinly sliced green onions

3 cups [120 g] finely chopped fresh cilantro leaves and tender stems

2 cups [80 g] finely chopped fresh parsley leaves

1 cup [40 g] finely chopped fresh dill leaves and tender stems

12 large eggs

2 Tbsp all-purpose flour

2 tsp kosher salt

1½ tsp ground turmeric

¼ tsp freshly ground black pepper

Fresh mint leaves, for garnish (optional)

Continued

Preheat the oven to 375°F [190°C] and set an oven rack in the middle position.

In a large nonstick skillet, heat 1 Tbsp of the oil over medium-high heat. Add the spinach and green onions and cook until softened and wilted, about 2 minutes. Transfer to a large bowl and let cool for 10 minutes. Add the cilantro, parsley, and dill and stir to combine.

In another bowl, whisk the eggs until lightly beaten. Add the flour, salt, turmeric, and pepper and whisk until smooth. Pour the mixture into the bowl with the herbs and stir until combined.

Add the remaining 3 Tbsp of oil to a 9 in [23 cm] square pan and tilt the pan to coat the bottom and sides. Pour the egg mixture into the pan and transfer to the oven. Bake until the eggs are just set, about 30 minutes.

Let cool for at least 10 minutes before cutting into 16 squares. Serve warm or at room temperature. Garnish with mint leaves before serving, if desired. Store, refrigerated, in a Stasher bag or an airtight container for up to 3 days.

ECO TIP Instead of buying single-serving and packaged snacks, make your own! Snacks like crackers and granola are easy things to whip up with a few ingredients (see pages 52 and 40 for recipes).

MAKES 16 BARS

Apple Streusel Bars

 Vegetarian   Make Ahead

STREUSEL

1¼ cups [210 g]
all-purpose flour

1 cup [120 g] old-fashioned
rolled oats

½ cup [100 g] packed light
brown sugar

¾ tsp kosher salt

10 Tbsp [140 g] unsalted
butter, cut into 10 pieces,
at room temperature

¼ cup [30 g] hazelnuts

¼ tsp ground cinnamon

Continued

Preheat the oven to 375°F [190°C]. Line the bottom and sides of an 8 in [20 cm] square baking dish with a parchment sling by folding two 8 by 16 in [20 by 40.5 cm] sheets of parchment paper, placing the parchment sheets perpendicular to each other in the dish, and leaving about 2 in [5 cm] of overhang on both sides. Brush lightly with oil or spray with vegetable oil spray.

To make the streusel, place the flour, oats, brown sugar, and salt in a food processor and pulse to combine. Add the butter and pulse until the mixture is the texture of coarse crumbs. Transfer ¾ cup [95 g] of the mixture to a bowl and reserve for the topping.

Pour the remaining mixture into the prepared pan and press down firmly to form an even crust. Bake until golden brown, about 20 minutes. Let cool on a wire rack for 10 minutes.

Continued

FILLING

2 Tbsp unsalted butter

1½ lb [680 g] apples,
peeled, cored, and sliced
⅛ in [4 mm] thick (about
5 cups)

2 Tbsp light brown sugar

½ tsp ground cinnamon

⅛ tsp ground nutmeg

⅓ cup [100 g] apricot jam

Meanwhile, to make the filling, in a large nonstick skillet over medium heat, melt the butter. Add the apples, brown sugar, cinnamon, and nutmeg and cook until the apples are tender and lightly browned, about 15 minutes. Remove from the heat and stir in the apricot jam. Spread the apples evenly over the crust and press down firmly to compact the mixture.

Place the hazelnuts in the food processor and pulse until coarsely chopped. Add the reserved streusel mixture and the cinnamon and pulse to combine. Pinch the mixture to form clumps, then sprinkle it on top of the apples. Bake until the streusel is golden brown, 20 to 25 minutes. Let cool completely on a wire rack. Remove the bars using the parchment sling and cut into 16 pieces. Store the bars in an airtight container in the refrigerator for up to 3 days.

MAKES 3 CUPS [150 G]

Everything Bagel Chips

 Vegetarian Make Ahead School-Lunch Friendly

1½ tsp sesame seeds

1½ tsp poppy seeds

1½ tsp dried minced onion

1½ tsp dried minced garlic

½ tsp coarse sea salt

2 day-old plain or other savory bagels

2 Tbsp extra-virgin olive oil

Preheat the oven to 325°F [165°C] and set an oven rack in the middle position. Line a baking sheet with parchment paper.

In a small bowl, combine the sesame seeds, poppy seeds, dried onion, dried garlic, and sea salt.

Using a knife, cut the bagels in half crosswise, then place them flat-side down and slice them into ¼ in [6 mm] thick planks. Cut these into triangle-shaped wedges.

Place the bagel pieces in a medium bowl and drizzle with the olive oil, tossing to coat. Sprinkle with the seasoning and toss again.

Transfer the bagel pieces to the prepared baking sheet in a single layer. Bake until golden brown, 20 to 25 minutes, turning the pieces over halfway through baking.

Let cool completely on the baking sheet or wire rack before transferring to an airtight container. Store at room temperature for up to 1 week.

ECO TIP Instead of throwing out overripe, brown bananas (which are safe to eat), store them in the freezer (leave the peels on until you're ready to use them, as the peel acts as a natural protective barrier against freezer burn). Incorporate the frozen bananas into smoothies and quickbread recipes, where their color and softness won't be noticed.

MAKES 2 CUPS [480 ML] (ENOUGH FOR 2 SNACK PORTIONS)

Peanut Butter Banana Oat Smoothie

 Vegetarian

1 frozen ripe banana

1 cup [240 ml] nondairy milk, such as oat, almond, or soy milk

¼ cup [25 g] old-fashioned rolled oats

2 Tbsp ground flaxseed

2 Tbsp Creamy Peanut Butter (page 64)

1 tsp honey

Pinch kosher salt (optional)

Let the banana thaw on the countertop for 10 minutes. Meanwhile, place the remaining ingredients in a blender.

Slice off the tips of the unpeeled banana, then cut the banana in half crosswise. Score the skin lengthwise on both sides of the banana halves, then peel the banana and place it in the blender.

Blend on high speed until smooth and creamy, about 30 seconds. Serve immediately or transfer to an insulated bottle or the refrigerator for up to 4 hours. Shake or stir before serving.

MAKES 35 CRACKERS

Cheddar-Onion Slice & Bake Crackers

 Vegetarian   Make Ahead   School-Lunch Friendly

1 cup [140 g] all-purpose flour

1 tsp kosher salt

1 tsp onion powder

½ tsp freshly ground black pepper

4 Tbsp unsalted butter, at room temperature, cut into ½ in [12 mm] pieces

4 oz [115 g] extra-sharp Cheddar cheese, coarsely grated, about 1 cup

1½ oz [40 g] cream cheese, cut into ½ in [12 mm] pieces (about ¼ cup)

Place the flour, salt, onion powder, and pepper in a food processor. Pulse until combined. Add the butter and pulse until the mixture resembles coarse meal. Add the Cheddar and cream cheese and process until the mixture forms a ball.

Turn the dough out onto a large sheet of parchment paper and roll into a tight log about 2 in [5 cm] in diameter. Wrap the dough in the parchment paper and refrigerate for at least 2 hours and up to 2 days.

Preheat the oven to 350°F [180°C] and set the racks in the upper and lower thirds of the oven. Line two baking sheets with parchment paper.

Continued

Cut the dough into ⅛ to ¼ in [4 to 6 mm] thick slices, rotating the log every few slices. Arrange the slices about 1 in [2.5 cm] apart on the prepared baking sheets. Bake until the crackers are golden brown, 12 to 15 minutes, rotating the baking sheets from front to back and top to bottom halfway through.

Set the baking sheets onto wire racks and let the crackers cool completely. Store the crackers in an airtight container at room temperature for up to 5 days.

MAKES 2 CUPS [185 G]

Crispy Barbecue Chickpeas

 Vegetarian   Make Ahead   Building Blocks   School-Lunch Friendly

Two 15½ oz [445 g] cans chickpeas, rinsed and drained

¼ cup [60 ml] extra-virgin olive oil

2 tsp smoked paprika

1 tsp brown sugar

1 tsp onion powder

½ tsp garlic powder

½ tsp kosher salt

¼ tsp mustard powder

¼ tsp ground cumin

¼ tsp freshly ground black pepper

Preheat the oven to 475°F [240°C]. Line a baking sheet with a folded dish towel. Line another baking sheet with parchment paper.

Place the chickpeas on the towel-lined baking sheet and let drain for 10 minutes, shaking the pan occasionally to aid moisture absorption.

Transfer the drained chickpeas to a large bowl. Add the oil, tossing until evenly coated. Transfer the chickpeas to the prepared baking sheet, shaking the pan gently so the chickpeas lie in an even layer. Set the bowl aside for later use (do not wash the bowl). Bake the chickpeas for 20 minutes, stirring once halfway through baking.

Continued

Lower the oven temperature to 350°F [180°C] and bake until the chickpeas are crisp and golden brown, 40 to 45 minutes, stirring once halfway through baking.

While the chickpeas bake, prepare the barbecue spice powder: In a small bowl, stir together the paprika, brown sugar, onion powder, garlic powder, salt, mustard powder, cumin, and pepper until combined.

Return the chickpeas to the bowl used earlier and toss to coat with the residual oil. Sprinkle the barbecue spice powder on top and toss until evenly coated. Return the chickpeas to the baking sheet and let cool completely, about 30 minutes. Store the chickpeas in a Stasher bag or an airtight container for up to 1 week.

SAUCES & CONDIMENTS

Flavorful Spreads and Toppings
to Enhance Every Dish

ECO TIP   When you find yourself with leftover or extra onion that needs to get used, slice and caramelize it to use for sandwiches (page 96), bowls (page 119), salads, pasta, or pizza.

MAKES ½ CUP [145 G]

Balsamic Caramelized Onions

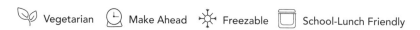 Vegetarian   Make Ahead   Freezable   School-Lunch Friendly

2 Tbsp extra-virgin olive oil

2 medium yellow onions, about 1¼ lb [570 g] total, thinly sliced

1 tsp fresh thyme leaves

½ tsp kosher salt

2 Tbsp balsamic vinegar

Heat the oil in a Dutch oven or large straight-sided skillet over medium heat. Add the onions and cook until they soften and become translucent, about 6 minutes, stirring occasionally.

Add the thyme and salt, lower the heat to medium-low, cover, and continue cooking until the onions are deeply browned and very soft, about 30 minutes, uncovering the pan to stir every few minutes. When the bottom of the pan starts getting brown, add ¼ cup [60 ml] of water and scrape up the browned bits from the bottom of the pan; the liquid will be reabsorbed into the onions. This step may be repeated, if necessary.

Uncover the pan, add the vinegar, and continue to cook until the onions are thick and sticky, about 6 minutes.

Transfer the onions to a large plate and let cool completely, then transfer to a Stasher bag or airtight container and refrigerate for up to 1 week. For longer storage, freeze in ice cube trays in 2 Tbsp increments.

MAKES 1 CUP [140 G]

Carrot, Radish & Fennel Pickles

 Vegetarian   Make Ahead

¼ cup [60 ml] white distilled vinegar

2 Tbsp granulated sugar

2 tsp kosher salt

⅓ cup [40 g] thinly sliced carrots

⅓ cup [50 g] thinly sliced radishes

⅓ cup [35 g] thinly sliced fennel

Place the vinegar, ¼ cup [60 ml] of water, the sugar, and salt in a small saucepan and bring to a simmer over medium heat. Stir until the sugar dissolves, about 1 minute.

Place the carrots, radishes, and fennel in a Stasher bag or glass jar. Pour the pickling liquid on top. Let cool to room temperature, then cover and refrigerate for up to 1 week.

Variation

Try using other crunchy vegetables, such as daikon, beets, red onion, bell peppers, and cucumber. They can be combined or pickled separately.

MAKES ABOUT 2 CUPS [520 G]

Creamy Peanut Butter

 Vegetarian   Make Ahead    Building Blocks

4 cups [560 g] unsalted
roasted peanuts

1 tsp kosher salt

Preheat the oven to 350°F [180°C]. Place the peanuts on a rimmed baking sheet.

Bake the peanuts until they are lightly browned and glistening with oil, about 10 minutes, stirring once half-way through baking. Transfer the peanuts and salt to a food processor and process until it forms a thick and creamy paste, about 4 minutes, stopping occasionally to scrape the bottom and sides of the work bowl.

Scrape the peanut butter into a Stasher bag or a glass jar. Store in the refrigerator for up to 2 months.

Variations

CREAMY NUT BUTTER: Swap in other nuts and seeds in lieu of the peanuts. Whether you use raw or pre-roasted nuts, be sure to toast them in the oven until lightly browned and fragrant. This process helps bring out and warm the oils, which aids processing.

HONEY NUT BUTTER: Add 1 Tbsp of honey at the end and process until combined.

CHUNKY NUT BUTTER: Reserve ½ cup [70 g] of coarsely chopped nuts and pulse them back into the creamy nut butter at the end.

MAKES 1 CUP [240 G]

Herbed Whipped Cream Cheese

 Vegetarian   Make Ahead   School-Lunch Friendly

8 oz [230 g] cream cheese, at room temperature

2 Tbsp milk

¼ tsp kosher salt

¼ tsp freshly ground black pepper

2 Tbsp chopped fresh basil leaves

2 Tbsp chopped fresh chives

1 Tbsp chopped fresh dill

1 tsp grated lemon zest

Place the cream cheese, milk, salt, and pepper in a food processor. Process until the mixture is whipped and creamy, about 30 seconds. Add the basil, chives, dill, and lemon zest and pulse to combine.

Transfer to a Stasher bag or glass jar and refrigerate for up to 1 week.

Variations

ROASTED GARLIC AND HERB: Replace the lemon zest with several cloves of smashed roasted garlic.

MAPLE CINNAMON: Replace 1 Tbsp of the milk with maple syrup and add ¼ tsp of cinnamon in place of the lemon zest and herbs.

ECO TIP Rather than buying herbs wrapped in plastic, start an herb garden in your kitchen or on your patio. You'll save money and reduce waste by growing your own herbs—plus they make for nice décor on your windowsill. Basil, rosemary, thyme, and sage are easy herbs to grow at home. They also make an awesome bouquet to take to a friend's house—flowers they can use!

MAKES 1 CUP [180 G]

Nut-Free Basil Pesto

 Vegetarian   Make Ahead   Freezable   Building Blocks   School-Lunch Friendly

¼ cup [35 g] pepitas, toasted

1 medium garlic clove

¾ tsp kosher salt

2½ cups [50 g] firmly packed basil leaves

½ cup [120 ml] extra-virgin olive oil

½ cup [15 g] grated Parmesan cheese

1 Tbsp lemon juice

1 tsp finely grated lemon zest

Place the pepitas, garlic, and salt in a food processor. Pulse until coarsely chopped. Add the basil and olive oil and process until smooth. Add the Parmesan cheese, lemon juice, and lemon zest and pulse until combined.

Use immediately, or freeze in ice cube trays in 2 Tbsp increments for up to 2 months.

Variation

Customize your pesto by using different nuts in place of the pepitas, experimenting with other soft-stemmed herbs or greens, such as arugula or watercress, to replace some or all of the basil, and swapping in another hard cheese, like Pecorino Romano, for the Parmesan.

MAKES 1½ CUPS [380 G]

White Bean Hummus

 Vegetarian   Make Ahead  Building Blocks

One 15½ oz [445 g] can
cannellini beans, rinsed
and drained

1 small garlic clove,
minced

1½ tsp kosher salt

¼ tsp ground cumin

¼ cup [55 g] tahini

¼ cup [60 ml] extra-virgin
olive oil

3 Tbsp fresh lemon juice

Place the beans, garlic, salt, and cumin in a food
processor and process until coarsely ground. Add
¼ cup [60 ml] of water, the tahini, olive oil, and lemon
juice, and process until smooth and creamy, about
2 minutes, stopping to scrape the bottom and sides
of the work bowl as needed.

Transfer to a Stasher bag or glass jar and refrigerate
for up to 1 week.

Variation

For flavored hummus, try adding some chopped
sun-dried tomatoes, roasted bell pepper strips,
cooked kale leaves, or roasted garlic cloves, and
process them along with the liquid ingredients.
For a more traditional hummus, use chickpeas
instead of cannellini beans.

SOUPS & SALADS

Fresh and Filling, These Dishes
Take Lunch to the Next Level

ECO TIP Eating seasonally and locally reduces your carbon footprint, as the produce travels a shorter distance to get to your plate. Stick to citrus fruits, pomegranates, kale, Brussels sprouts, and radishes in the winter, and indulge in stone fruits, berries, tomatoes, corn, and zucchini in the summer.

SERVES 2

Baked Tofu Salad with Miso-Sesame Vinaigrette

 Vegetarian Make Ahead Building Blocks School-Lunch Friendly

MISO-SESAME VINAIGRETTE

2 Tbsp rice vinegar

1 Tbsp white miso paste

2 tsp maple syrup

½ tsp grated ginger

¼ tsp kosher salt

3 Tbsp canola oil

1 Tbsp toasted sesame oil

Continued

To make the dressing, in a small bowl, whisk together the vinegar, miso paste, maple syrup, ginger, and salt until smooth. Add the canola and sesame oils and whisk until emulsified.

Continued

BAKED TOFU SALAD

⅔ cup [105 g] Baked Tofu (page 31)

¼ cup [55 g] Carrot, Radish & Fennel Pickles (page 63)

1 mandarin orange, peeled and segmented

¼ cup [35 g] sliced English cucumber

½ cup [80 g] cooked shelled edamame

¼ [35 g] cup thinly sliced radishes

4 cups [140 g] torn red leaf lettuce

1 Tbsp toasted sesame seeds

To assemble the salad, divide the ingredients between two lunch containers or Stasher bags in the following order: tofu, pickles, orange segments, cucumber, edamame, radishes, lettuce, and sesame seeds. Pour 2 Tbsp of the dressing per serving into two small containers or Stasher Pocket bags. Transfer the remaining dressing into a glass jar and refrigerate for up to 2 days.

Variations

SUMMERTIME TOFU: Replace the mandarin orange with cherry tomatoes and the fresh radishes with corn.

PAN-FRIED TOFU: For a crispier tofu, prepare the tofu as described on pages 31–32, but instead of arranging it on a baking sheet, heat 1 Tbsp of olive oil in a large shallow sauté pan over medium heat. Using tongs, add the tofu pieces to the pan in a single layer. Sauté, turning the tofu pieces over until they are crispy on all sides.

ECO TIP Don't throw that stale bread in the trash! There are tons of things you can do with bread once it's past its prime. You can make croutons, as below, thicken up soups (page 88), or bake them into chips (page 48).

SERVES 2

Chicken Caesar Salad with Parmesan Croutons

 Make Ahead   Building Blocks   School-Lunch Friendly

PARMESAN CROUTONS

¼ cup [60 ml] extra-virgin olive oil

1 garlic clove, smashed

3 cups [90 g] ½ in [12 mm] crustless bread cubes, torn from day-old bread

2 Tbsp grated Parmesan cheese

Kosher salt

Continued

To make the croutons, in a large skillet, heat the olive oil over medium heat. Add the garlic and sauté until golden and fragrant, about 2 minutes. Add the bread cubes and cook, stirring occasionally, until browned and crisp, about 4 minutes. Discard the garlic. Stir in the Parmesan cheese and season with salt to taste. Transfer to a baking sheet and let cool completely.

Continued

CAESAR DRESSING

¼ cup [60 g] mayonnaise

1 Tbsp fresh lemon juice

1 Tbsp Dijon mustard

1 tsp Worcestershire sauce

1 anchovy fillet, minced

1 tsp kosher salt

½ tsp honey

¼ tsp freshly ground black pepper

¼ cup extra-virgin olive oil

2 Tbsp grated Parmesan cheese

CAESAR SALAD

⅔ cup [85 g] shredded roast chicken

¼ cup [35 g] thinly sliced radishes

4½ cups [200 g] chopped romaine lettuce

¼ cup [25 g] shaved Parmesan cheese (optional)

To make the dressing, in a medium bowl, whisk together the mayonnaise, lemon juice, mustard, Worcestershire sauce, anchovy, salt, honey, and pepper until combined. Add the olive oil and Parmesan cheese and whisk until emulsified.

To pack the salad, divide the ingredients between two lunch containers or Stasher bags in the following order: chicken, radishes, lettuce, and Parmesan, if desired. Pour 2 Tbsp of the dressing per serving into two small containers or Stasher Pocket bags. Pack ¼ cup [10 g] croutons per serving in two small containers or Stasher Pocket bags. Transfer the remaining dressing to a glass jar and refrigerate for up to 3 days. Store leftover croutons in a Stasher bag or an airtight container at room temperature for up to 2 days.

ECO TIP Rather than throwing away your food scraps—such as stalks, leaves, and tops from your veggies, or the bones from your chicken or turkey—store the vegetable and meat scraps in separate freezer bags (like a Stasher Half Gallon) until you have enough for a base. Then use them to make a rich and satisfying stock (see page 32).

SERVES 4

Chicken Noodle Soup

 Make Ahead ❄ Freezable ✓ Building Blocks 🗃 School-Lunch Friendly

1 Tbsp olive oil

1 small onion, diced

1 carrot, thinly sliced

1 celery stalk, thinly sliced

1 tsp fresh thyme leaves

5 cups [1.2 L] chicken stock or 4 cups [960 ml] stock plus 1 cup [240 ml] water

4 oz [115 g] pasta, cooked until al dente (about 2 cups)

1⅓ cups [170 g] shredded roast chicken

2 Tbsp minced parsley leaves

Kosher salt and freshly ground black pepper

In a large saucepan, warm the oil over medium-high heat. Add the onion, carrot, and celery and cook until softened, about 3 minutes. Add the thyme. Add the chicken stock and bring to a boil. Lower the heat to medium and simmer, partially covered, until the vegetables are just tender, about 10 minutes. At this point, you can cool and refrigerate the soup base overnight or continue as follows if serving the same day.

Stir in the cooked pasta and chicken and simmer until warmed through, about 1 minute. Stir in the parsley and season to taste with salt and pepper. Pack hot into insulated, vacuum-sealed lunch containers or let cool completely before refrigerating and reheating. Leftovers will keep in the refrigerator for 1 day and in the freezer for up to 1 month.

ECO TIP Salad greens can go bad quickly if you don't store them properly. To avoid ending up with soggy, slimy, sad greens, wrap them in a cotton dish towel and place them in a Stasher bag—the towel will absorb excess moisture and the Stasher bag will keep them fresher longer.

SERVES 2

Cobb Salad with Chicken & Avocado Dressing

 Make Ahead   Building Blocks

AVOCADO DRESSING

½ avocado, peeled and pitted

¼ cup [3 g] fresh flat-leaf parsley leaves

¼ cup [3 g] fresh basil leaves

¼ cup [12 g] roughly chopped green onion or chives

2 Tbsp fresh lemon juice

2 Tbsp extra-virgin olive oil

1 small garlic clove

1 anchovy fillet

1 tsp kosher salt

Continued

To make the dressing, place all the ingredients plus 6 Tbsp [90 ml] of water in a blender. Blend on high speed until creamy.

To pack the salad, divide the ingredients between two lunch containers or Stasher bags in the following order: roast chicken, ham, tomatoes, corn, eggs, radishes, lettuce, and cheese. Pour 3 Tbsp of the dressing per serving into two small containers or Stasher Pocket bags. Transfer the remaining dressing into a glass jar and refrigerate for up to 2 days.

Continued

COBB SALAD

⅔ cup [85 g] shredded
roast chicken

2 oz [55 g] cubed ham
steak or thinly sliced deli
ham

½ cup [80 g] halved cherry
tomatoes

½ cup [80 g] cooked corn
kernels

2 hard-boiled eggs, peeled
and halved

¼ cup [35 g] thinly sliced
radishes

4 cups [140 g] chopped
romaine lettuce

¼ cup [30 g] crumbled
blue cheese

Variation

SPRING SALAD: For a springtime variation, replace the
cherry tomatoes and corn with chopped blanched
asparagus and sugar snap peas, and the ham with
crisped prosciutto.

ECO TIP Replace almonds, pistachios, walnuts, and pecans with more eco-friendly nut options, like hazelnuts, brazil nuts, cashews, and peanuts, which are more sustainable to grow and process. They are packed with nutrients and protein, and they use less water resources during the farming and processing stages. Seeds, such as sunflower, pumpkin, and sesame, have an even smaller water footprint!

SERVES 2

Kale Salad with Apples, Lentils, Feta & Seeds

 Vegetarian   Make Ahead   Building Blocks

APPLE CIDER VINAIGRETTE

¼ cup [60 ml] apple cider vinegar

2 Tbsp minced shallot

2 Tbsp Dijon mustard

2 tsp maple syrup

1 tsp kosher salt

½ cup [120 ml] canola oil

Continued

To make the vinaigrette, in a medium bowl, whisk together the vinegar, shallot, mustard, maple syrup, and salt until combined. Add the oil and whisk until emulsified.

Continued

KALE SALAD

1 cup [200 g] cooked green or brown lentils

½ cup [60 g] crumbled feta cheese

1 small Gala, Fuji, or Honeycrisp apple, cored and thinly sliced

4½ cups [70 g] thinly sliced kale

¼ cup [35 g] roasted shelled sunflower seeds

To make the salad, in a large bowl, combine the lentils with 6 Tbsp [90 ml] of the vinaigrette (the lentils will dress the entire salad). The remaining vinaigrette will keep in a glass jar in the refrigerator for up to 2 days.

To assemble the salad, divide the ingredients between two lunch containers or Stasher bags in the following order: dressed lentils, feta, apple slices, kale, and sunflower seeds. If preparing the salad the night before, don't add the sunflower seeds until the next morning.

ECO TIP   Instead of tossing a loaf that's past its prime, you can use stale bread to make croutons or breadcrumbs. Stale bread can also be used for French toast, bread pudding, or to thicken soups.

SERVES 4

Italian Tomato-Bread Soup

 Vegetarian   Make Ahead   Freezable    School-Lunch Friendly

3 Tbsp extra-virgin olive oil

1 small onion, finely chopped

3 garlic cloves, minced

One 28 oz [800 g] can whole peeled tomatoes

2 tsp kosher salt, plus more as needed

¼ tsp freshly ground black pepper, plus more as needed

3 cups [90 g] torn day-old country bread (1 in [2.5 cm] pieces)

2 Tbsp chopped basil

1 to 2 tsp sugar (optional)

Parmesan Croutons, for serving (page 77)

In a large pot, heat the olive oil over medium heat. Add the onion and cook until softened, about 8 minutes, adding the garlic in the last minute.

While the onion cooks, transfer the tomatoes (reserve the juices in the can) to a bowl and crush them by hand into coarse chunks. Add the tomatoes, salt, and pepper to the onion and garlic, increase the heat to medium-high, and cook until thickened, 6 to 8 minutes. Stir in the bread pieces, tomato juices, 4 cups [960 ml] of water, and the basil, and bring to a boil. Lower the heat to medium and simmer, whisking occasionally to break down the bread, until the soup has a thick, porridge-like consistency, about 10 minutes. Season to taste with more salt and pepper, and add the sugar, if needed, to balance the acidity.

Pack hot into insulated, vacuum-sealed lunch containers or let cool completely before refrigerating. Leftovers will keep in the refrigerator for 1 day and in the freezer for 1 month. Pack 2 Tbsp of the Parmesan Croutons per serving into Stasher Pocket bags for garnish.

Variation

For a kid-friendly version, reduce the amount of bread to 1 cup [30 g] and stir in 2 cups [400 g] of cooked orzo, macaroni, or alphabet pasta during the last 2 minutes of cooking.

SANDWICHES

Bagels, Wraps, and More to Satisfy
Every Lunch Craving

SERVES 2

Pesto Chicken Sandwich

 Building Blocks ☐ School-Lunch Friendly

1 cup [130 g] shredded roast chicken

2 Tbsp Nut-Free Basil Pesto (page 68) or prepared pesto

2 Tbsp chopped oil-packed sun-dried tomatoes

2 Tbsp mayonnaise

4 slices whole wheat sandwich bread

2 slices provolone cheese

¼ cup [55 g] roasted red bell pepper strips

In a medium bowl, combine the chicken and pesto; set aside.

In a small bowl, stir together the sun-dried tomatoes and mayonnaise.

Spread the sun-dried tomato mayonnaise onto each slice of bread. Top the bottom bread slices with cheese, followed by the pesto chicken and bell pepper strips. Cover with the remaining bread slices, mayo-side down, to close each sandwich. Pack each sandwich in a Stasher bag, a hard-sided container, or reusable wrap.

SERVES 2

Chickpea Waldorf Salad on Lavash

 Vegetarian   Make Ahead   Building Blocks

¼ cup [60 g] mayonnaise

2 tsp fresh lemon juice

1 tsp Dijon mustard

One 15½ oz [445 g] can chickpeas, rinsed and drained

½ cup [80 g] halved red grapes

¼ cup [35 g] diced red onion

¼ cup [30 g] diced celery

¼ cup [30 g] peeled and diced Fuji or Gala apple

Kosher salt and freshly ground black pepper

¼ cup [35 g] roasted sunflower seeds

2 sheets lavash

4 leaves red or green leaf lettuce, washed and dried

In a medium bowl, combine the mayonnaise, lemon juice, and mustard. Add the chickpeas and lightly crush with a fork until about half are smashed. Stir in the grapes, onion, celery, and apple. Season to taste with salt and pepper. Refrigerate in an airtight container for up to 2 days.

Divide the salad between two sealed containers or Stasher bags and sprinkle the sunflower seeds on top. Divide the lavash and lettuce leaves between two containers or Stasher bags. At lunchtime, place a lettuce leaf and some of the salad on the lavash and roll up gently.

Variations

CURRIED CHICKPEA SALAD: Add toasted curry powder to the mayonnaise mixture.

PITA POCKETS: For a kid-friendly version, use 2 pita breads, halved. Place a lettuce leaf inside each pita pocket and fill with salad.

ECO TIP For a meat-free option and a lower
carbon footprint, swap the roast beef
for a veggie patty.

SERVES 2

Roast Beef Sandwiches

 Make Ahead   School-Lunch Friendly

3 Tbsp mayonnaise

1 Tbsp prepared
horseradish or whole-
grain mustard

2 ciabatta rolls, split

2 Tbsp Balsamic
Caramelized Onions
(page 60)

4 oz [115 g] deli-sliced
roast beef

2 slices extra-sharp
Cheddar cheese, about
½ oz [15 g] each

½ cup [10 g] baby arugula

In a small bowl, stir together the mayonnaise and
horseradish and spread on the cut sides of the
rolls. Spread 1 Tbsp of the caramelized onions
onto the bottom of each roll, then top with the
beef and cheese. Cover with the top halves of
the rolls. Wrap the sandwiches in reusable
wrap or pack in a Stasher bag the night before
and store them in the refrigerator.

Divide the arugula into two small containers or
Stasher Pocket bags to add to the sandwich
just before serving.

Variations

HONEY MUSTARD DRESSING: To make this sandwich
more kid friendly, use honey mustard in place
of the horseradish and omit the arugula.

MUSHROOM SANDWICH: For a veggie version,
replace the roast beef with grilled portobello
mushroom caps marinated in soy sauce, olive
oil, and balsamic vinegar.

ECO TIP Don't throw out that leftover avocado half! Save it for another sandwich, bowl, or salad the next day, or use it in the Avocado Dressing (page 82). If you can't get to it right away, brush the exposed flesh with lemon juice and freeze it in a Stasher bag; thaw the frozen avocado and use it in smoothies, creamy dips and dressings, and even quickbreads.

SERVES 2

Hummus & Roasted Veggie Wraps

 Vegetarian  Building Blocks  School-Lunch Friendly

½ cup [125 g] White Bean Hummus (page 71)

¼ tsp smoked paprika

Two 10 in [25 cm] flour tortillas

2 cups [300 to 430 g] assorted diced roasted vegetables, such as sweet potatoes, zucchini, mushrooms, and bell peppers

¼ cup [5 g] baby spinach

¼ cup [40 g] Carrot, Radish & Fennel Pickles (page 63), drained and blotted dry

½ ripe avocado, sliced

In a small bowl, stir together the hummus and paprika.

Spread the hummus evenly over the tortillas, leaving a ½ in [12 mm] border. Arrange the roasted vegetables, spinach, pickles, and avocado onto the lower third of the tortilla. Roll up the tortilla tightly, like a burrito.

Wrap the sandwiches in parchment paper and seal with a piece of tape or secure with a rubber band.

ECO TIP When you're buying fish, always check the label or ask the person at the counter to find out where your fish is coming from. Seafoodwatch.org is a great resource for information on sustainable, eco-conscious seafood.

SERVES 2

Salmon Sandwiches with Herbed Cream Cheese

 Make Ahead   School-Lunch Friendly

SOUS VIDE SALMON

Two 4 to 5 oz [115 to 140 g] wild salmon fillets, 1 in [2.5 cm] thick or less

1 Tbsp whole-grain mustard

1 tsp kosher salt

½ tsp honey

1 Tbsp extra-virgin olive oil

Continued

To make the salmon, fill a large pot with warm water and set a sous vide machine to 120°F [50°C] to pre-heat the water bath.

Meanwhile, in a small bowl, combine the mustard, salt, and honey to form a paste. Apply the mustard paste all over the fillets and place them side by side in a large Stasher bag. Drizzle the olive oil into the bag. To remove as much air as possible from the bag, seal it three-quarters of the way, then slowly lower the bag into the water, holding the opened end above the water. Before the bag is completely submerged, seal the rest of the bag.

Cook for 30 to 45 minutes, using binder clips or weights to keep the bags submerged, if necessary.

Remove the bag from the water and place it in a large bowl filled with ice water until the salmon is chilled. Assemble the sandwich immediately, or refrigerate the salmon for up to 2 days.

2 bagels, sliced and lightly toasted

⅓ cup [80 g] Herbed Whipped Cream Cheese (page 67)

4 thin slices tomato

¼ cup [55 g] Carrot, Radish & Fennel Pickles (page 63), drained and blotted dry

½ cup [10 g] baby arugula

To assemble the sandwiches, spread the cream cheese onto the cut sides of the bagels. Place the salmon, tomato, and pickles in between the bagel halves. Pack the sandwiches in reusable wrap, a hard-sided container, or a Stasher bag. Divide the arugula between two small containers or Stasher Pocket bags to add to the sandwich just before eating.

ECO TIP Set up a compost bin, toss in any unusable scraps (such as eggshells and coffee grounds), and use the resulting fertilizer in your flowerbeds (coffee shops will give away coffee grounds to add to your compost too). Many municipalities in urban areas offer curbside pickup for compost. Keep a small covered bin on your counter or in your freezer (to reduce the smell), and take it out regularly.

SERVES 2

Spinach-Feta Frittata Sandwich

 Vegetarian Make Ahead

1 tsp olive oil

4 large eggs

¼ tsp kosher salt

¼ tsp freshly ground black pepper

1 small shallot, thinly sliced

½ cup [120 g] cooked spinach

¼ cup [30 g] crumbled feta cheese

2 Tbsp mayonnaise

2 Tbsp Nut-Free Basil Pesto (page 68) or prepared pesto

Two 4 in [10 cm] squares focaccia

4 thin slices tomato

Continued

Fill a stockpot halfway with water and bring to a boil.

Drizzle the oil into a sandwich-size Stasher bag and massage the bag until evenly coated.

Place the eggs, salt, and pepper in a medium bowl and whisk to combine. Stir in the shallot, spinach, and feta.

Pour the egg mixture into the Stasher bag. Squeeze most of the air out of the bag and seal it tightly. Drop the Stasher bag into the boiling water and let it cook until the frittata is set, about 15 minutes. Make sure the bag remains submerged as it cooks.

Use tongs to remove the bag from the boiling water. Let cool for 1 minute, then carefully open the bag and let the frittata slide out onto a cutting board. Let cool until barely warm, then proceed as follows if eating right away, or return the frittata to the bag and refrigerate overnight.

Mix the mayonnaise and pesto in a small bowl. Split the focaccia pieces horizontally to make 4 thinner, sandwich-size slices. Spread the mayonnaise mixture onto the cut sides of the focaccia halves. Cut the frittata in half crosswise. Sandwich each piece of frittata and 2 tomato slices between 2 slices of focaccia. Pack the sandwiches in reusable wrap, a hard-sided container, or a Stasher bag.

GRAINS & PASTAS

Satisfying and Hearty Dishes to Nourish You,
No Matter What the Day Throws Your Way

SERVES 3

Act 2 Fried Rice

 Make Ahead   Building Blocks   School-Lunch Friendly

5 tsp [25 ml] vegetable oil

¼ cup [35 g] finely chopped carrot

¼ cup [35 g] finely chopped onion, shallot, or green onion

½ cup [60 g] frozen peas, edamame, or corn

½ cup [60 g] chopped vegetables (previously cooked or raw)

½ cup [65 g] bite-size pieces of leftover cooked meat, shrimp, or tofu

1 garlic clove, minced

3 cups [440 g] cooked rice

1 egg, lightly beaten

Kosher salt

2 tsp soy sauce, tamari, fish sauce, or other salty condiment

1 tsp toasted sesame oil

In a large nonstick skillet, warm 2 tsp of the vegetable oil over medium-high heat. Add the carrot and onion and cook until starting to soften, about 2 minutes. Add the frozen peas and vegetables and cook for 2 minutes more. Add the leftover meat and cook until lightly browned, about 2 minutes, adding the garlic halfway through cooking. Transfer to a bowl.

Add 2 tsp more of the vegetable oil to the skillet and heat over medium-high heat. Add the rice and smash it down into an even layer. Let cook, undisturbed, for 2 minutes. Stir the rice and cook for 1 minute more without stirring. Season the egg with salt. Push the rice to one side of the skillet and add the remaining 1 tsp of vegetable oil to the other side. Add the egg and cook, stirring frequently with a spatula, until barely set, about 10 seconds. Quickly stir the rice and egg together, breaking the egg apart into small pieces.

Add the soy sauce, sesame oil, and cooked vegetable-meat mixture and stir-fry for 2 minutes. Season to taste with additional salt. Pack hot into insulated, vacuum-sealed lunch containers or let cool completely before refrigerating and reheating. Leftovers will keep in the refrigerator for up to 2 days.

SERVES 2

Tuna Pesto Pasta Salad with Tomatoes & Beans

 Make Ahead ⊘ Building Blocks ▢ School-Lunch Friendly

2 cups [400 g] cooked fusilli or penne pasta

¼ cup [45 g] Nut-Free Basil Pesto (page 68) or prepared pesto

½ cup [80 g] halved cherry tomatoes

½ cup [90 g] chopped blanched green beans

One 5 oz [140 g] can tuna, drained and flaked

Extra-virgin olive oil

Kosher salt and freshly ground black pepper

Grated Parmesan cheese, for serving (optional)

In a bowl, stir together the pasta and pesto until evenly coated. Add the tomatoes, green beans, and tuna and toss until combined. Drizzle with olive oil and season to taste with salt and pepper. Sprinkle Parmesan cheese on top, if desired.

Divide between two lunch containers or Stasher bags and refrigerate for up to 1 day.

ECO TIP When shopping for deli meats, rather than buying prepackaged slices, go to the deli counter and purchase only as much as you need. Bring a Stasher bag to store the meat in rather than using the plastic bag from the market.

SERVES 2

Orzo with Ham & Buttered Peas

 Building Blocks   School-Lunch Friendly

½ cup [85 g] orzo

½ cup [60 g] frozen peas

1 Tbsp extra-virgin olive oil

2 Tbsp unsalted butter

1 Tbsp minced shallot

2 oz [55 g] deli ham, cut into thin strips

¼ cup [8 g] grated Parmesan cheese

Kosher salt and freshly ground black pepper

Bring a small saucepan of water to a boil over high heat. Add the orzo and cook until al dente, about 9 minutes, adding the peas during the last 3 minutes of cooking. Drain in a sieve and transfer to a bowl. Add the olive oil and stir to coat.

Add the butter to the saucepan and melt over medium heat. Add the shallot and ham and cook until the shallot is soft and translucent, about 2 minutes. Return the orzo and peas to the pan and stir in the cheese. Season to taste with salt and pepper. Pack hot into insulated, vacuum-sealed lunch containers.

SERVES 2

Chicken Fajita Bowl

 Make Ahead   Building Blocks   School-Lunch Friendly

GUACAMOLE

½ avocado, peeled, pitted, and diced

2 Tbsp chopped cilantro leaves and tender stems

1 Tbsp fresh lime juice

¼ tsp kosher salt

Pinch red pepper flakes

¼ cup [40 g] chopped cherry tomatoes

Continued

To make the guacamole, in a small bowl, mash together the avocado, cilantro, lime juice, salt, and red pepper flakes (or you can add the ingredients to a large Stasher bag, seal the bag, and smash the bag with your hands—kids love this!). Fold in the tomatoes.

Continued

FAJITA BOWL

1 Tbsp vegetable oil

½ small onion, sliced

½ red bell pepper, cut into ¼ in [6 mm] strips

1 garlic clove, minced

⅛ tsp ground cumin

⅛ tsp kosher salt

1½ cups [135 to 180 g] cooked grain of your choice

½ cup [65 g] shredded roast chicken

½ cup [80 g] cooked black beans

½ cup [80 g] cooked corn kernels

½ cup [40 g] chopped romaine lettuce

¼ cup [20 g] shredded Monterey Jack or Cheddar cheese

Hot sauce, for serving (optional)

To make the fajita bowls, in a medium skillet, heat the oil over medium-high heat. Add the onion and bell pepper and sauté until tender-crisp, 7 to 8 minutes. Add the garlic, cumin, and salt and cook until fragrant, about 1 minute.

To assemble, divide the grains into two lunch containers or Stasher bags, then arrange the onion-pepper mixture, chicken, beans, corn, lettuce, and cheese on top. Divide the guacamole between two small containers or Stasher Pocket bags; add to the bowl just before serving. Serve with hot sauce, if desired.

SERVES 2

Brown Rice, Lentils & Greens Bowl with Glazed Cashews

 Vegetarian   Make Ahead   Building Blocks

GLAZED CASHEWS

¼ cup [35 g] roasted cashews

1 Tbsp honey

⅛ tsp ground cumin

Kosher salt and freshly ground black pepper

Continued

To make the glazed cashews, place the cashews, 1 Tbsp of water, the honey, cumin, a pinch of salt, and a pinch of pepper in a small saucepan and bring to a simmer over medium heat. Cook, stirring frequently, until a golden-brown glaze coats the nuts, about 5 minutes. Transfer to a plate and let cool completely.

Continued

BROWN RICE AND LENTIL BOWL

1 cup [200 g] cooked green or brown lentils

2 Tbsp vinaigrette (page 33)

2 Tbsp Balsamic Caramelized Onions (page 60)

1½ cups [250 g] cooked brown rice (page 27)

½ cup [65 g] sautéed hearty greens, such as kale, Swiss chard, or collard greens

½ cup [75 g] roasted diced sweet potatoes

¼ cup [60 g] White Bean Hummus (page 71), thinned with 1 Tbsp water

To assemble the bowls, stir together the lentils, vinaigrette, and caramelized onions in a medium bowl.

Divide the rice between two lunch containers or Stasher bags, then arrange the seasoned lentils, greens, and sweet potatoes on top. Drizzle the thinned hummus over everything. Pack the cashews into two small containers or Stasher Pocket bags; scatter over the bowls just before serving.

SERVES 2

Vegetarian Quinoa Bibimbap Bowl

 Vegetarian   Make Ahead   Building Blocks

2 tsp soy sauce

1 tsp toasted sesame oil

1 tsp toasted sesame seeds

½ tsp granulated sugar

2 tsp vegetable oil

4 oz [115 g] shiitake mushrooms, stemmed and sliced

1 carrot, peeled and cut into thin matchsticks

6 oz [170 g] baby spinach

1 garlic clove, minced

Kosher salt

1½ cups [180 g] cooked quinoa (page 27)

1 cup [150 g] Baked Tofu (page 31)

¼ cup [55 g] kimchi or Carrot, Radish & Fennel Pickles (page 63)

1 green onion, thinly sliced

2 tsp gochujang paste, thinned with water to a drizzling consistency

In a small bowl, stir together the soy sauce, sesame oil, sesame seeds, and sugar. Set aside.

In a large nonstick skillet, warm 1 tsp of the vegetable oil over medium-high heat. Add the mushrooms and cook until tender and lightly browned, about 4 minutes. Add the carrot and cook until softened, about 3 minutes. Remove from the heat and stir in the soy sauce mixture. Transfer to a bowl.

Heat the remaining 1 tsp of oil in the skillet over medium-high heat. Add the spinach and cook until wilted, about 2 minutes. Add the garlic and cook until fragrant, about 1 minute. Season with salt to taste.

Divide the quinoa between two lunch containers or Stasher bags, then arrange the mushroom-carrot mixture, spinach, tofu, kimchi, and green onion on top. Drizzle with the thinned gochujang paste.

Variation

EXTRA SPICY BOWL: For a spicier version, just add your favorite hot sauce or chili sauce to the gochujang paste.

Litter-Free
Life

Simple Ways to Reduce Waste
at Home & Beyond

Now that you're
a litter-free lunch
pro, let's take things
up a notch! We put
together this guide
to a litter-free life
to make it easier
for you to practice
plastic-free habits
no matter where
you are.

AT HOME

Room by room, rethink where you can reuse or repurpose products and eliminate single-use plastic options. Some of our favorite places to start:

1. BATHROOM

Try a bamboo toothbrush (when it's come to the end of its life, the bristles need to be tossed in the garbage, but the handle can be composted).

Opt for paper-wrapped toilet paper and paper towels.

Choose refill sizes of soaps and cleaning products instead of a new spray bottle or soap dispenser.

Try toothpaste tablets instead of buying plastic tubes.

Use a shampoo bar instead of plastic bottles.

Reuse ribbons from gifts to dress up pigtails and ponytails.

2. PANTRY

Choose products (such as nut butters) in reusable glass jars instead of plastic.

Forget those tear-off plastic baggies in the produce section and toss your loose veggies in a reusable shopping bag instead.

PRO TIP *Group like produce items together during checkout to save your cashier a little time!*

3.

Repurpose shallow storage containers that have lost their lids and control the clutter in your junk drawers.

Switch to powdered laundry detergent in a cardboard box instead of plastic jugs of liquid detergent.

PRO TIP *Powdered detergent looks great in a decorative glass container or extra-large mason jar on your countertop!*

4.

GARAGE

Instead of tossing plastic bags, reuse them to sort and store spring bulbs, fertilizer, loose nuts/bolts, and so on.

Repurpose cardboard shipping boxes to organize holiday decorations, sporting equipment, and camping cookware.

5.

CLOSETS

Need new hangers? Choose wood instead of plastic.

Repurpose cardboard shipping boxes to store seasonal clothes or grow-into sizes of hand-me-downs.

6.

KIDS' ROOMS

Store arts and crafts supplies in reusable bags, closable plastic storage containers, or repurposed bins, so they're easy to find.

Give disposable plastic bags another hurrah by storing toys by type or set.

Reuse old egg cartons to help organize tiny doll accessories, game pieces, hair ties, and the like.

PRO TIP *Store sets of building bricks in separate, labeled bags with the instructions included!*

GIFT GIVING

Take thoughtful gifting to a whole new level!

1. **REUSE**

Instead of buying gift wrap, wrap presents in newspaper, old calendars, or fabric scraps.

Make your own gift certificate and skip the plastic gift card.

Reuse ribbons and gift bags— save money and the planet!

PRO TIP *Store gift bags by occasion or color so that it's easy to grab what you need, and store smaller bags within larger bags.*

2. **EXPERIENCE**

Give experiences, not stuff: Skip the things that may turn into clutter, and instead give a lunch date, movie tickets, or plan an outing in nature.

3. **DONATE**

Donate to Mother Earth: What better way to save the planet than by donating to a nonprofit organization in your friend's name?

4. **BAKE**

They say that the quickest way to the heart is through the stomach— and nothing beats homemade! From baking a fresh batch of goodies for friends to surprising a loved one with their favorite meal, a personal touch always makes for a memorable gift.

OUT & ABOUT

When you're out and about in the world, keep this mantra in mind:
Reduce—reuse—repurpose/rethink/refuse—recycle. Then rinse and repeat.

1.
OUT TO EAT
Bring a reusable bag to the bakery or sandwich shop to carry your purchase.

Pack a reusable utensil kit and skip single-use straws, spoons, forks, and other disposables.

Keep a reusable bag or container handy for leftovers when dining out, and refuse the to-go box.

Bring your own insulated travel mug to the coffee shop.

2.
OUT WITH PETS
Store treats in reusable bags that become your pet's favorite thing EVER.

Keep biodegradable poop bags and a collapsible reusable water dish with your dog's leash and treats for sustainable walks.

3.
OUT WITH KIDS
Keep a stash of past-their-prime plastic bags to store dirty diapers until they can make it to a trash can.

Pack a reusable waterproof bag for dirty clothing.

Pack reusable cloths for wiping kids' faces and hands, rather than relying on disposable wipes.

4.
WORKING OUT
Keep a reusable, resealable bag to store sweaty gym clothes or a wet swimsuit.

Pair a reusable water bottle with your gym bag so they're never apart, and you're never dehydrated (or tempted to buy bottled water).

ADVENTURE & TRAVEL

Practice "Leave No Trace" wherever you go—if you pack it in, then pack it out.
And bonus points if you leave a place even cleaner than you found it.
(Learn more about Leave No Trace principles at LNT.org.)

1. CONTAINERS

Store your travel-size liquid containers in a reusable, resealable bag (might we suggest a Stasher bag in sandwich or half-gallon [2 L] size?).

Instead of using the hotel's bathroom products (usually packaged in plastic), bring your own refillable containers with your favorite suds. If you have to use the little bottles at the hotel, pack them up and take them with you for your next trip.

2. PACKAGING

Give dry cleaning or plastic garment bags another life by packing them between layers of clothes in your suitcase to reduce wrinkles.

3. DIY KITS

Make your own first aid kit (the premade ones are usually full of unnecessary plastic). Fill a sturdy bag or container with bandages, pain medication, bug spray, antibiotic ointment, blister guards, and so on.

4. SNACKS

If you need snacks for a road trip or adventure, forgo prepackaged trail mix and freeze-dried snacks in plastic packaging and pack your own trail mix, dried fruit, or cereal bars in an airtight container.

5. AT THE BEACH

Instead of using single-use bags to keep your phone protected from water or sand, tuck it into a Stasher bag; you can still use the touch screen through the silicone!

RESOURCES

Habits are easier to keep when you're having fun and staying true to your passions. And because there's no one way to love our planet, all you have to do is pick your favorite! Whether you're a foodie, an avid hiker, a wildlife enthusiast, or a beach lover, or you just want to reduce your footprint—here are some terrific organizations to keep you inspired on your litter-free journey. These are resources we love and look to for helpful info, eco insights, charged-up missions, and more.

1% FOR THE PLANET

A great resource for choosing brands that are giving back to the environment, this org has donated over $225 million to highly vetted environmental nonprofits. Stasher is a proud supporter!
www.onepercentfortheplanet.org

5 GYRES

5 Gyres empowers action through science, education, and adventure. They're walking the walk with research expeditions in all five subtropical gyres and clean-up efforts across the world's lakes and rivers.
www.5gyres.org

CONSERVATION INTERNATIONAL

This global org works to protect the natural resources we rely on for our food, fresh water, and livelihoods. All contributions support science, policy work, and partnerships aimed at solving the climate crisis.
www.conservation.org

FASHION REVOLUTION

Love fashion and fairness? Fashion Revolution unites people and brands to work toward creating a safer, cleaner industry.
www.fashionrevolution.org

FOOD RECOVERY NETWORK

Waste not, want not. This org supports initiatives on college campuses across the United States to significantly reduce food waste and end hunger.
www.foodrecoverynetwork.org

LEAVE NO TRACE

Learn how to love our parks and protected spaces responsibly with research and education from the Center for Outdoor Ethics.
www.LNT.org

NO KID HUNGRY

No Kid Hungry is an organization devoted to ending child hunger in America. Through school initiatives, community partnerships, family education, and advocacy, No Kid Hungry helps children get the healthy food they need every day—whether or not school is in session.
www.nokidhungry.org

ONE TREE PLANTED

It's simple. One dollar = one tree. Help support reforestation organizations around the world that are working to stabilize the climate and provide habitats. You can even become a Tree Ambassador in your own community!
https://onetreeplanted.org

SURFRIDER

Surfrider works to protect water quality, beach preservation, and marine and coastal ecosystems through local campaigns, community initiatives, and legislation.
www.surfrider.org

WORLD WILDLIFE FUND

The world's leading conservation org, WWF works in more than 100 countries to help people and nature thrive. Their site offers quick, easy, high-impact ways to get involved.
www.worldwildlife.org

How else do you live a litter-free life? Let us know—
we love hearing your ideas, inspiration, and accomplishments!
Keep us posted @stasherbag. #LitterFreeLife

STASHER'S 30-DAY CHALLENGE

After you've flipped through these pages and discovered your favorite recipes and tips, head on over to stasherbag.com/30daychallenge to take your plastic-free living to the next level with weekly checklists, how-tos, and more inspiration. Then follow @stasherbag on Instagram for some community love and to show off your cooking skills.

"Individually,
we are one drop.
Together, we are
an ocean."

—RYUNOSUKE SATORO

THANK-YOUS

A NOTE FROM STASHER'S FOUNDER, KAT NOURI

As an entrepreneur and mother, Stasher was my expression of hope for the future, rooted in my strong belief that change is possible. Today, I stand in awe of what we have created together. In just a few short years, we've disrupted an entire industry, achieved exponential growth, and found an enthusiastic community that shares our passion for protecting the planet. To all of you in the Stasher Squad: Thank you for believing in a mission-based company, for spreading the word, and for doing your part each and every day. Our planet's bright future belongs to those who Save What Matters.

As the old saying goes, behind every good man is a good woman! The same is true in reverse. Behind this woman is an amazing man. I love you Sal/Afshin for believing in my crazy ideas, holding me up, pushing me forward, and helping me raise our babies. I got to have my family and strive to my fullest potential—I didn't have to choose between life and mission-driven work because they so seamlessly blended together. And to our kids, Koosha, Kian, Denna, Kandace, and Lilo, I'm so glad you've gotten to be a part of building the business. After all, you share this entrepreneurial DNA. I'm also grateful for my incredible mom, Sonia, and her emotional and financial support, which has been beyond measure, and my dad, Gus, for encouraging all of my big dreams. Thanks also to my brother, Nasser, for your big heart and for believing in me, and to my best friend/sister, Laili, for all your support and love! And to Ahmed and Reem for helping me become a socially and environmentally conscious entrepreneur. To Mike Fake, my CFO, my friend, my rock. Katie Reinman, your grace and hard work is unforgettable. And to the original Stasher Squad, you are the best team on the planet!

I am so grateful that I've been able to do what I love every day, help create positive impact, and be part of something much bigger than myself. It's all more than I could have ever dreamed of. Thank you, thank you, thank you.

INDEX

KAT NOURI is an entrepreneur, an avid homecook, and the founder of Stasher. As a mother of three, she wanted to provide her family with healthy, eco-friendly meals and also protect them from harmful chemicals found in plastic packaging. That's why she created Stasher—reusable silicone storage bags—to give families everywhere a safe, accessible, daily alternative to single-use plastics.

STASHER is on a mission to help create a plastic-free lifestyle. By offering endlessly reusable alternatives to single-use plastics and radically functional solutions to reinvent food storage, the Stasher Squad is dedicated to leaving the planet better than we found it. Founded in 2016 by Kat Nouri, the company is based in Emeryville, California.

stasher
save what matters™